MANGA SHAKESPEARE®

AS YOU LIKE IT

ADAPTED BY
RICHARD APPIGNANESI

ILLUSTRATED BY
CHIE KUTSUWADA

Published by
SelfMadeHero
A division of Metro Media Ltd
5 Upper Wimpole Street
London W1G 6BP
www.selfmadehero.com

This edition published 2008

Illustrator: Chie Kutsuwada
Text Adaptor: Richard Appignanesi
Designer: Andy Huckle
Textual Consultant: Nick de Somogyi
Editorial Assistant: Jane Laporte
Publishing Director: Emma Hayley

ISBN-13: 978-0-9558169-0-1

10 9 8 7 6 5 4 3 2 1
Printed and bound in China

The Forest of Ar-Den, a place of magical transformation...
"O poor Orlando, thou art overthrown!"
Orlando, youngest son of Rowland de Boys
"That thou didst know how many fathom deep I am in love!"
Rosalind, daughter of the rightful Duke Senior – alias Ganymede

"Firm and irrevocable is my doom!"
Duke Frederick, Duke Senior's tyrannical older brother
Celia, the daughter of Duke Frederick – alias Aliena
"My father's envious disposition sticks me at heart!"

Old Adam, Orlando's faithful servant
"O, what a world is this!"
"I never loved my brother in my life!"
Oliver, Orlando's tyrannical eldest brother

"All the world's a stage!"
Jaques, a melancholy lord in Duke Senior's retinue
Duke Senior, exiled to Ar-Den by his usurping brother Frederick
"Sweet are the uses of adversity!"

Audrey, a country goat-herd
"The gods give us joy!"
"As all is mortal, so is all love folly!"
Touchstone, Rosalind's Fool

"Sweet Phoebe,
do not scorn me!"

Silvius, a country swain

Phoebe, a country girl

"If sight
and shape
be true...!"

Corin, a humble shepherd

"I know the property
of rain is to wet,
and fire to burn..."

Charles, a wrestler at Duke Frederick's court
"Tomorrow I wrestle for my credit. . ."
Jaques de Boys, brother of Orlando and Oliver
"I bring tidings to this fair assembly. . ."
"Peace, ho! 'Tis I must make conclusion!"
Hymen, the God of Marriage

"Here's eight that
must take hands...
to join in Hymen's bands!"

AS I REMEMBER, ADAM, IT WAS BEQUEATHED ME BY WILL A THOUSAND CROWNS TO BREED ME WELL.
MY BROTHER KEEPS ME RUSTICALLY AT HOME.
HIS HORSES ARE BRED BETTER.

THE SPIRIT OF MY FATHER, WHICH IS WITHIN ME, BEGINS TO MUTINY AGAINST THIS SERVITUDE.
I WILL NO LONGER ENDURE IT!
YONDER COMES MY MASTER, YOUR BROTHER.

SHALL I KEEP YOUR HOGS, AND EAT HUSKS WITH THEM?
KNOW YOU WHERE YOU ARE, SIR?
HERE IN YOUR ORCHARD.
KNOW YOU BEFORE WHOM, SIR?

I KNOW YOU ARE MY ELDEST BROTHER, AND, IN THE GENTLE CONDITION OF BLOOD, YOU SHOULD SO KNOW ME.
WILT THOU LAY HANDS ON ME, VILLAIN?
I HAVE AS MUCH OF MY FATHER IN ME AS YOU.

I AM THE YOUNGEST SON OF SIR ROWLAND DE BOYS, AND HE IS THRICE A VILLAIN THAT SAYS SUCH A FATHER BEGOT VILLAINS.
WERT THOU NOT MY BROTHER, I WOULD NOT TAKE THIS HAND FROM THY THROAT TILL THIS OTHER HAD PULLED OUT THY TONGUE FOR SAYING SO.
FOR YOUR FATHER'S REMEMBRANCE, BE AT ACCORD.

LET ME GO, I SAY.
MY FATHER CHARGED YOU IN HIS WILL TO GIVE ME GOOD EDUCATION.
YOU HAVE TRAINED ME LIKE A PEASANT.
I WILL NO LONGER ENDURE IT.
THEREFORE ALLOW ME SUCH EXERCISES AS MAY BECOME A GENTLEMAN,
OR GIVE ME THE ALLOTTERY MY FATHER LEFT ME BY TESTAMENT.

AND WHAT WILT THOU DO?
BEG, WHEN THAT IS SPENT?
YOU SHALL HAVE SOME PART OF YOUR WILL.
LEAVE ME.
GET YOU WITH HIM, YOU OLD DOG.
IS "OLD DOG" MY REWARD?
MY OLD MASTER WOULD NOT HAVE SPOK
SUCH A WORD.

BEGIN YOU TO GROW UPON ME?
I WILL PHYSIC YOUR RANKNESS AND GIVE NO THOUSAND CROWNS NEITHER.
GOOD MORROW TO YOUR WORSHIP.
CHARLES, WHAT'S THE NEW NEWS AT THE NEW COURT?

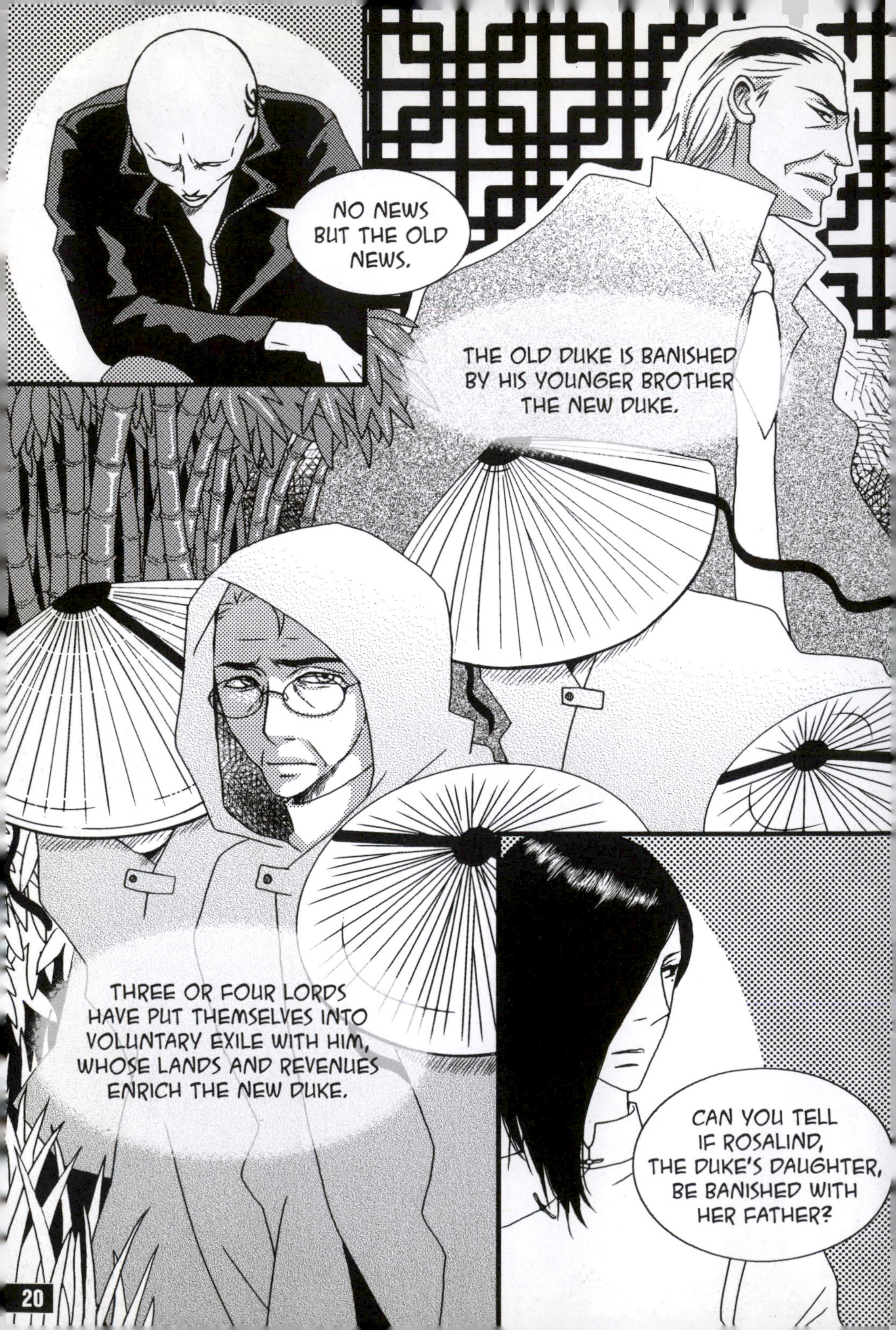
NO NEWS BUT THE OLD NEWS.
THE OLD DUKE IS BANISHED BY HIS YOUNGER BROTHER THE NEW DUKE.
THREE OR FOUR LORDS HAVE PUT THEMSELVES INTO VOLUNTARY EXILE WITH HIM, WHOSE LANDS AND REVENUES ENRICH THE NEW DUKE.
CAN YOU TELL IF ROSALIND, THE DUKE'S DAUGHTER, BE BANISHED WITH HER FATHER?

O, NO, FOR THE DUKE'S DAUGHTER, HER COUSIN, SO LOVES HER, SHE WOULD HAVE FOLLOWED HER EXILE OR HAVE DIED TO STAY BEHIND HER.
NEVER TWO LADIES LOVED AS THEY DO.

WHERE WILL
THE OLD DUKE LIVE?
THEY SAY HE IS ALREADY IN THE FOREST OF AR-DEN, AND MANY MERRY MEN WITH HIM.
THEY LIVE LIKE THE OLD ROBIN HOOD, IN THE GOLDEN WORLD.
YOU WRESTLE TOMORROW BEFORE THE NEW DUKE?

MARRY DO I, SIR.
I AM GIVEN TO UNDERSTAND THAT YOUR BROTHER ORLANDO HATH A DISPOSITION TO COME IN AGAINST ME.
TOMORROW I WRESTLE FOR MY CREDIT, AND HE THAT ESCAPES ME WITHOUT SOME BROKEN LIMB SHALL ACQUIT HIM WELL.
SWISH

SNATCH
OUT OF MY LOVE TO YOU,
I CAME HITHER THAT YOU MIGHT STAY HIM FROM HIS INTENDMENT.
I HAD MYSELF NOTICE OF MY BROTHER'S PURPOSE, AND HAVE LABOURED TO DISSUADE HIM FROM IT...
BUT HE IS RESOLUTE.
THEREFORE USE THY DISCRETION.
I HAD AS LIEF THOU DIDST BREAK HIS NECK AS HIS FINGER.
CLICK!

FOR, I ASSURE THEE — AND ALMOST WITH TEARS I SPEAK IT — THERE IS NOT ONE SO VILLAINOUS THIS DAY LIVING.
I SPEAK BUT BROTHERLY OF HIM; BUT SHOULD I ANATOMIZE HIM TO THEE AS HE IS, I MUST BLUSH AND WEEP...
AND THOU MUST LOOK PALE AND WONDER.
I AM HEARTILY GLAD I CAME HITHER TO YOU.
IF HE COME TOMORROW, I'LL GIVE HIM HIS PAYMENT.

AND SO GOD KEEP YOUR WORSHIP!
FAREWELL, GOOD CHARLES.
NOW I SHALL SEE AN END OF HIM!
FOR MY SOUL, I KNOW NOT WHY, HATES NOTHING MORE THAN HE.

YET HE'S GENTLE, NEVER SCHOOLED AND YET LEARNED,
OF ALL SORTS ENCHANTINGLY BELOVED, SO MUCH ESPECIALLY OF MY OWN PEOPLE, THAT I AM ALTOGETHER MISPRIZED.
BUT IT SHALL NOT BE SO LONG.
THIS WRESTLER SHALL CLEAR ALL.

I PRAY THEE, ROSALIND, BE MERRY.

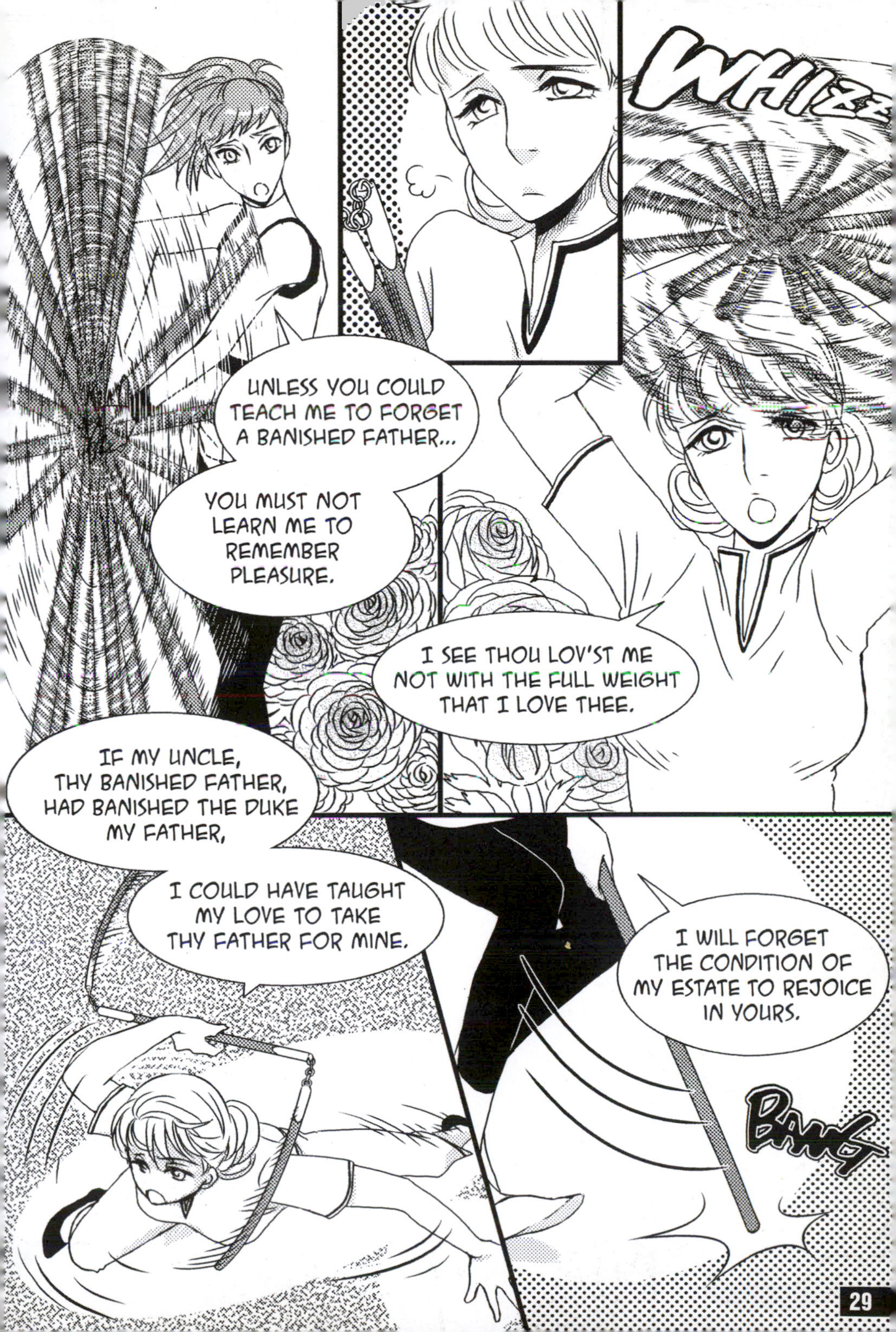
WHIZZ
UNLESS YOU COULD TEACH ME TO FORGET A BANISHED FATHER...
YOU MUST NOT LEARN ME TO REMEMBER PLEASURE.
I SEE THOU LOV'ST ME NOT WITH THE FULL WEIGHT THAT I LOVE THEE.
IF MY UNCLE, THY BANISHED FATHER, HAD BANISHED THE DUKE MY FATHER,
I COULD HAVE TAUGHT MY LOVE TO TAKE THY FATHER FOR MINE.
I WILL FORGET THE CONDITION OF MY ESTATE TO REJOICE IN YOURS.
BANG

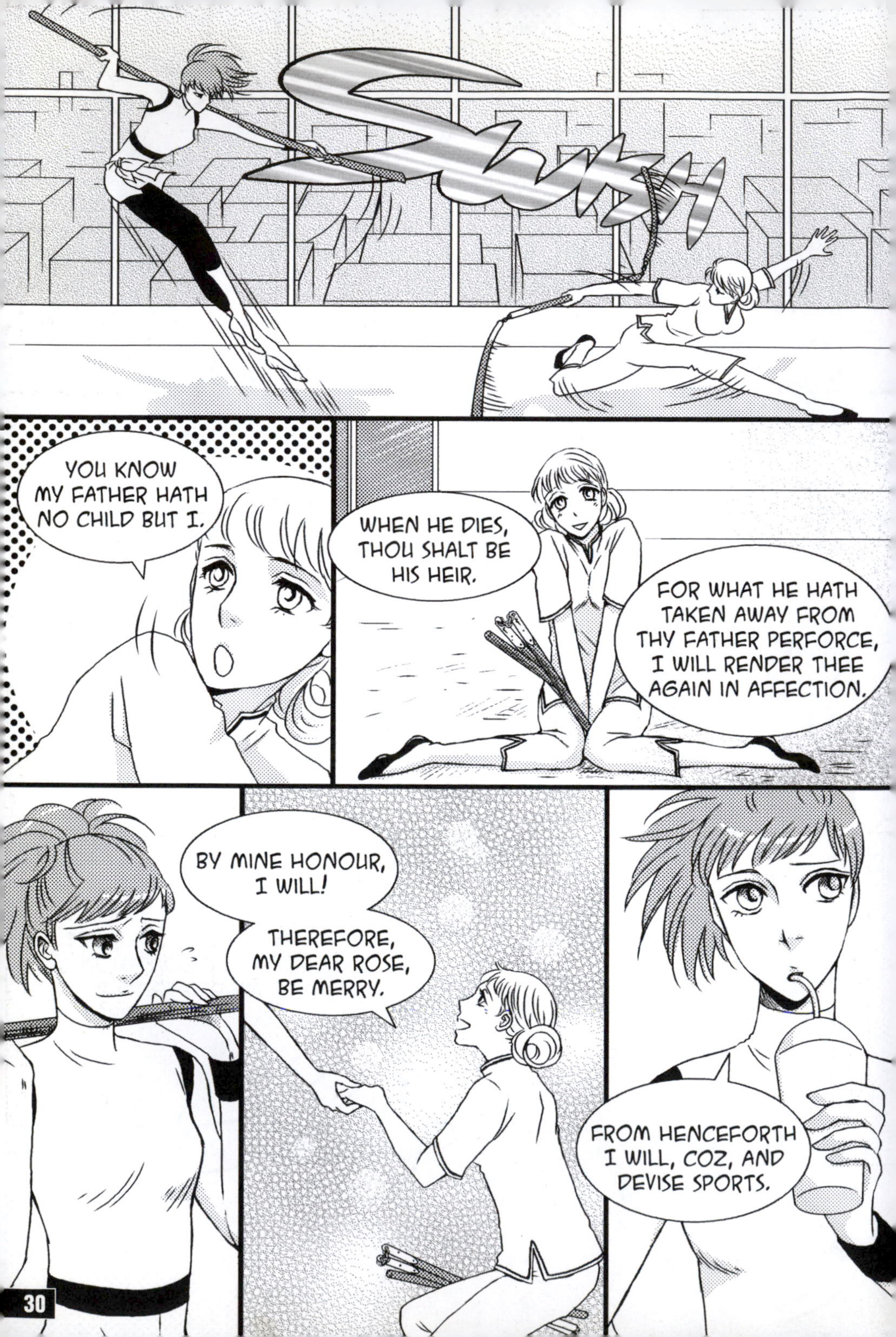
YOU KNOW MY FATHER HATH NO CHILD BUT I.
WHEN HE DIES, THOU SHALT BE HIS HEIR.
FOR WHAT HE HATH TAKEN AWAY FROM THY FATHER PERFORCE, I WILL RENDER THEE AGAIN IN AFFECTION.
BY MINE HONOUR, I WILL!
THEREFORE, MY DEAR ROSE, BE MERRY.
FROM HENCEFORTH I WILL, COZ, AND DEVISE SPORTS.

LET ME SEE: WHAT THINK YOU OF FALLING IN LOVE?
I PRITHEE, DO, TO MAKE SPORT WITHAL.
BUT LOVE NO MAN IN GOOD EARNEST.
WHAT SHALL BE OUR SPORT THEN?
LET US SIT AND MOCK THE GOOD HOUSEWIFE FORTUNE...
THAT HER GIFTS MAY HENCEFORTH BE BESTOWED EQUALLY.
I WOULD WE COULD DO SO, FOR HER BENEFITS ARE MIGHTILY MISPLACED.

'TIS TRUE; FOR HATH NOT FORTUNE SENT IN THIS FOOL TO CUT OFF THE ARGUMENT?
!
HOW NOW, WIT! WHITHER WANDER YOU?
MISTRESS, YOU MUST COME AWAY TO YOUR FATHER.
WERE YOU MADE THE MESSENGER?
NO, BY MINE HONOUR, BUT I WAS BID TO COME FOR YOU.

WHERE LEARNED YOU THAT OATH, FOOL?
TADA ~ ♫
OF A CERTAIN KNIGHT THAT SWORE BY HIS HONOUR.
HOW PROVE YOU THAT, IN THE GREAT HEAP OF YOUR KNOWLEDGE?
AY, NOW UNMUZZLE YOUR WISDOM.

STROKE YOUR CHINS,
AND SWEAR BY YOUR BEARDS THAT I AM A KNAVE.
BY OUR BEARDS, IF WE HAD THEM, THOU ART.
BY MY KNAVERY, IF I HAD IT...
THEN I WERE.
BUT IF YOU SWEAR BY THAT THAT IS NOT, YOU ARE NOT FORSWORN.
NO MORE WAS THIS KNIGHT, SWEARING BY HIS HONOUR, FOR HE NEVER HAD ANY.

PRITHEE, WHO IS'T THAT THOU MEAN'ST?
ONE THAT YOUR FATHER LOVES.
PING!
ENOUGH! SPEAK NO MORE OF HIM. YOU'LL BE WHIPPED ONE OF THESE DAYS.
THE MORE PITY, THAT FOOLS MAY NOT SPEAK WISELY WHAT WISE MEN DO FOOLISHLY.

BY MY TROTH, THOU SAYEST TRUE.
HERE COMES MONSIEUR LE BEAU.
WITH HIS MOUTH FULL OF NEWS.
FAIR PRINCESS, YOU HAVE LOST MUCH GOOD SPORT.
SPORT? OF WHAT COLOUR?

YOU AMAZE ME, LADIES.
I WOULD HAVE TOLD YOU OF GOOD WRESTLING, WHICH YOU HAVE LOST THE SIGHT OF.
YET TELL US THE MANNER OF THE WRESTLING.
I WILL TELL YOU THE BEGINNING; AND, IF IT PLEASE YOUR LADYSHIPS, YOU MAY SEE THE END, FOR THEY ARE COMING TO PERFORM IT.

THERE COMES AN OLD MAN, AND HIS THREE SONS OF EXCELLENT GROWTH AND PRESENCE –
DOM
THE ELDEST OF THE THREE WRESTLED WITH CHARLES, THE DUKE'S WRESTLER...
CHARLES BROKE THREE OF HIS RIBS.

BAM!
DOMP!
SO HE SERVED THE SECOND, AND SO THE THIRD.
YONDER THEY LIE, THEIR FATHER MAKING SUCH PITIFUL DOLE OVER THEM THAT ALL THE BEHOLDERS TAKE HIS PART WITH WEEPING.
IT IS THE FIRST TIME THAT EVER I HEARD BREAKING OF RIBS WAS SPORT FOR LADIES.
OR I, I PROMISE THEE.

PING
BUT IS THERE ANOTHER DOTES UPON RIB-BREAKING?
SHALL WE SEE THIS WRESTLING, COUSIN?
YOU MUST, IF YOU STAY HERE, FOR HERE THEY ARE READY TO PERFORM IT.
IS YONDER THE MAN?

EVEN HE, MADAM.
ALAS! HE IS TOO YOUNG.
HOW NOW, DAUGHTER AND COUSIN! ARE YOU CREPT HITHER TO SEE THE WRESTLING?
AY, MY LIEGE, SO PLEASE YOU GIVE US LEAVE.
YOU WILL TAKE LITTLE DELIGHT IN IT.

IN PITY OF
THE CHALLENGER'S YOUTH
I WOULD FAIN DISSUADE HIM.
BUT HE WILL NOT
BE ENTREATED.
SPEAK TO HIM, LADIES.
SEE IF YOU CAN
MOVE HIM.
CALL HIM HITHER,
GOOD MONSIEUR LE BEAU.

YOUNG GENTLEMAN, YOUR SPIRITS ARE TOO BOLD FOR YOUR YEARS.
YOU HAVE SEEN CRUEL PROOF OF THIS MAN'S STRENGTH.
WE PRAY YOU, FOR YOUR OWN SAKE, TO EMBRACE YOUR OWN SAFETY AND GIVE OVER THIS ATTEMPT.
DO, YOUNG SIR.

YOUR REPUTATION SHALL NOT THEREFORE BE MISPRIZED.
WE WILL MAKE IT OUR SUIT TO THE DUKE THAT THE WRESTLING MIGHT NOT GO FORWARD.
I CONFESS ME MUCH GUILTY TO DENY SO FAIR AND EXCELLENT LADIES ANYTHING.
BUT LET YOUR WISHES GO WITH ME TO MY TRIAL.
THE WORLD NO INJURY, FOR IN IT I HAVE NOTHING.
IF I BE FOILED, THERE IS BUT ONE SHAMED.
IF KILLED, BUT ONE DEAD THAT IS WILLING TO BE SO.
I SHALL DO MY FRIENDS NO WRONG, FOR I HAVE NONE TO LAMENT ME...

THE LITTLE STRENGTH THAT I HAVE, I WOULD IT WERE WITH YOU.
AND MINE, TO EKE OUT HERS.
FARE YOU WELL. PRAY HEAVEN I BE DECEIVED IN YOU!
YOUR HEART'S DESIRES BE WITH YOU!

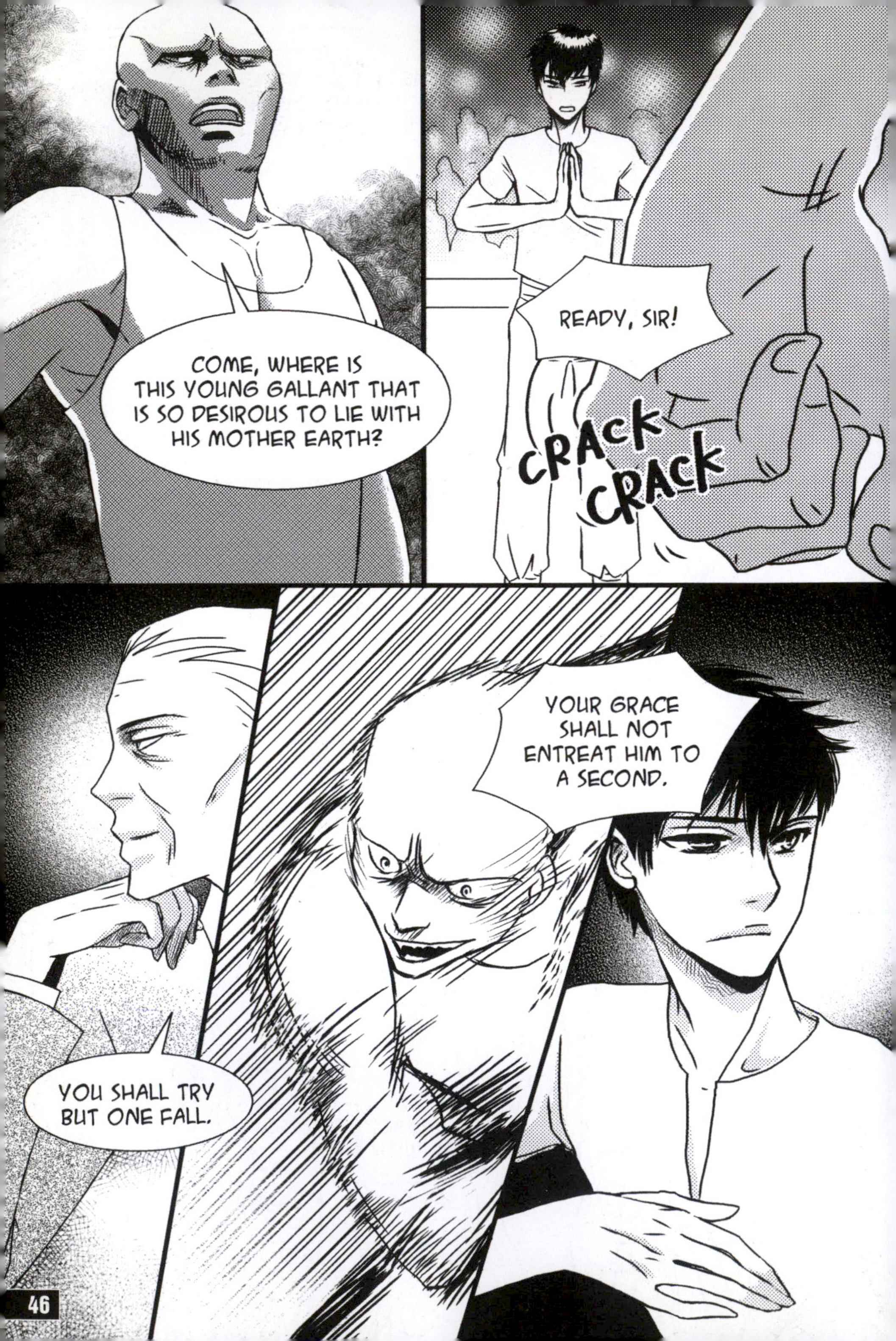
COME, WHERE IS THIS YOUNG GALLANT THAT IS SO DESIROUS TO LIE WITH HIS MOTHER EARTH?
READY, SIR!
CRACK CRACK
YOUR GRACE SHALL NOT ENTREAT HIM TO A SECOND.
YOU SHALL TRY BUT ONE FALL.

VISH!!
I WOULD I WERE INVISIBLE, TO CATCH THE STRONG FELLOW BY THE LEG.
SHH!
O EXCELLENT YOUNG MAN!
HWAAA

BAAASH!
PANT
PANT
PANT
PANT
PANT
HOW DOST THOU, CHARLES?
HELP
HE CANNOT SPEAK, MY LORD.

WHAT IS THY NAME, YOUNG MAN?
ORLANDO, MY LIEGE, THE YOUNGEST SON OF SIR ROWLAND DE BOYS.
I WOULD THOU HADST BEEN SON TO SOME MAN ELSE.
THE WORLD ESTEEMED THY FATHER HONOURABLE, BUT I DID FIND HIM STILL MINE ENEMY.
BUT FARE THEE WELL!
THOU ART A GALLANT YOUTH.

I AM MORE PROUD TO BE SIR ROWLAND'S SON, AND WOULD NOT CHANGE THAT CALLING TO BE ADOPTED HEIR TO FREDERICK.
MY FATHER LOVED SIR ROWLAND AS HIS SOUL, AND ALL THE WORLD WAS OF MY FATHER'S MIND.
MY FATHER'S ENVIOUS DISPOSITION STICKS ME AT HEART.

SIR, IF YOU DO KEEP YOUR PROMISES IN LOVE, AS YOU HAVE EXCEEDED ALL PROMISE,
YOUR MISTRESS SHALL BE HAPPY.
WEAR THIS FOR ME...
ONE THAT COULD GIVE MORE, BUT THAT HER HAND LACKS MEANS.
SHALL WE GO, COZ?
AY. FARE YOU WELL, FAIR GENTLEMAN.

CAN I NOT SAY, "I THANK YOU"?
THAT WHICH HERE STANDS UP IS BUT A MERE LIFELESS BLOCK.
...
DID YOU CALL, SIR?
SIR, YOU HAVE WRESTLED WELL, AND OVERTHROWN MORE THAN YOUR ENEMIES.

WILL YOU GO, COZ?
WHAT PASSION HANGS THESE WEIGHTS UPON MY TONGUE?
O POOR ORLANDO, THOU ART OVERTHROWN!
OR CHARLES OR SOMETHING WEAKER MASTERS THEE.

GOOD SIR, I DO IN FRIENDSHIP COUNSEL YOU TO LEAVE THIS PLACE.
SUCH IS NOW THE DUKE'S CONDITION THAT HE MISCONSTRUES ALL THAT YOU HAVE DONE.
WHAT HE IS INDEED MORE SUITS YOU TO CONCEIVE THAN I TO SPEAK OF.
I THANK YOU, SIR.
TELL ME THIS: WHICH OF THE TWO WAS DAUGHTER OF THE DUKE?
...

NEITHER HIS DAUGHTER, IF WE JUDGE BY MANNERS.
BUT INDEED, THE SMALLER IS HIS DAUGHTER.
THE OTHER IS DAUGHTER TO THE BANISHED DUKE...
AND HERE DETAINED BY HER USURPING UNCLE TO KEEP HIS DAUGHTER COMPANY...
WHOSE LOVES ARE DEARER THAN THE NATURAL BOND OF SISTERS.

BUT I CAN TELL YOU THAT OF LATE THIS DUKE HATH TAKEN DISPLEASURE AGAINST HIS GENTLE NIECE...
ON NO OTHER ARGUMENT BUT THAT THE PEOPLE PRAISE HER FOR HER VIRTUES, AND PITY HER FOR HER GOOD FATHER'S SAKE.
HIS MALICE AGAINST THE LADY WILL SUDDENLY BREAK FORTH.

SIR,
FARE YOU WELL.
HEREAFTER,
IN A BETTER WORLD THAN THIS,
I SHALL DESIRE MORE LOVE
AND KNOWLEDGE OF YOU.
I REST MUCH
BOUNDEN TO YOU.
FARE YOU WELL.
THUS MUST I
FROM THE SMOKE INTO
THE SMOTHER, FROM
TYRANT DUKE UNTO A
TYRANT BROTHER.
BUT HEAVENLY
ROSALIND!

ROSALIND!
CUPID HAVE MERCY!
NOT A WORD?
NOT ONE TO
THROW AT A DOG.
BUT IS ALL THIS
FOR YOUR FATHER?
O, HOW FULL OF
BRIERS IS THIS
WORKING-DAY WORLD!

COME, COME, WRESTLE WITH THY AFFECTIONS.
O, THEY TAKE THE PART OF A BETTER WRESTLER THAN MYSELF!
...
IS IT POSSIBLE, ON SUCH A SUDDEN, YOU SHOULD FALL INTO SO STRONG A LIKING WITH OLD SIR ROWLAND'S YOUNGEST SON?
BLUSH
WHIZ!

LOOK, HERE COMES THE DUKE.
WITH HIS EYES FULL OF ANGER.
MISTRESS, DISPATCH YOU WITH YOUR SAFEST HASTE, AND GET YOU FROM OUR COURT.
ME, UNCLE?
YOU, COUSIN.
WITHIN THESE TEN DAYS IF THAT THOU BE FOUND SO NEAR OUR PUBLIC COURT AS TWENTY MILES...
THOU DIEST FOR IT.

DEAR UNCLE!
NEVER SO MUCH AS IN A THOUGHT UNBORN DID I OFFEND YOUR HIGHNESS.
THUS DO ALL TRAITORS.
LET IT SUFFICE THEE THAT I TRUST THEE NOT.
YET YOUR MISTRUST CANNOT MAKE ME A TRAITOR.

THOU ART THY FATHER'S DAUGHTER.
THERE'S ENOUGH.
SO WAS I WHEN YOUR HIGHNESS TOOK HIS DUKEDOM.
SO WAS I WHEN YOUR HIGHNESS BANISHED HIM.
TREASON IS NOT INHERITED, MY LORD.
MY FATHER WAS NO TRAITOR.
THEN MISTAKE ME NOT SO TO THINK MY POVERTY IS TREACHEROUS.
DEAR SOVEREIGN, HEAR ME SPEAK.

AY, CELIA,
WE STAYED HER FOR YOUR SAKE.
ELSE HAD SHE WITH HER FATHER
RANGED ALONG.
IF SHE BE A TRAITOR,
WHY SO AM I.
WE HAVE SLEPT, LEARNED...
PLAYED, ATE TOGETHER.

WHERESOEVER WE WENT, LIKE JUNO'S SWANS, WE WENT COUPLED AND INSEPARABLE.
SHE IS TOO SUBTLE FOR THEE.
HER VERY SILENCE AND HER PATIENCE SPEAK TO THE PEOPLE, AND THEY PITY HER.
THOU WILT SHOW MORE BRIGHT AND SEEM MORE VIRTUOUS...
WHEN SHE IS GONE.

THEN OPEN NOT THY LIPS.
FIRM AND IRREVOCABLE IS MY DOOM –
SHE IS BANISHED!
PRONOUNCE THAT SENTENCE THEN ON ME, MY LIEGE.
I CANNOT LIVE OUT OF HER COMPANY.
YOU ARE A FOOL.
YOU, NIECE, IF YOU OUTSTAY THE TIME...
YOU DIE.

O MY POOR ROSALIND!
BE NOT MORE GRIEVED THAN I AM.
I HAVE MORE CAUSE.
THOU HAST NOT, COUSIN.
KNOW THOU NOT THE DUKE HATH BANISHED ME, HIS DAUGHTER?
THAT HE HATH NOT.

NO, HATH NOT?
SHALL WE PART, SWEET GIRL?
NO!
LET MY FATHER SEEK ANOTHER HEIR.
I'LL GO ALONG WITH THEE.
WHY, WHITHER SHALL WE GO?

TO SEEK MY UNCLE IN THE FOREST OF AR-DEN.
ALAS, WHAT DANGER WILL IT BE TO US, MAIDS AS WE ARE, TO TRAVEL FORTH SO FAR!
Ta dah!
I'LL PUT MYSELF IN POOR ATTIRE, AND SMIRCH MY FACE.
THE LIKE DO YOU.
SO SHALL WE PASS ALONG.

WERE IT NOT BETTER, BECAUSE I AM MORE THAN COMMON TALL, THAT I DID SUIT ME LIKE A MAN?
IN MY HEART, LIE THERE WHAT HIDDEN WOMAN'S FEAR THERE WILL...
WE'LL HAVE A MARTIAL OUTSIDE.

WHAT SHALL I CALL THEE WHEN THOU ART A MAN?
I'LL HAVE NO WORSE A NAME THAN JOVE'S OWN PAGE.
CALL ME GANYMEDE.
BUT WHAT WILL YOU BE CALLED?
NO LONGER CELIA, BUT ALIENA.

WHAT IF WE ASSAYED TO STEAL THE CLOWNISH FOOL OUT OF YOUR FATHER'S COURT?
WOULD HE NOT BE A COMFORT TO OUR TRAVEL?
?
!
HE'LL GO ALONG OVER THE WIDE WORLD WITH ME.
!
LET'S AWAY, AND GET OUR JEWELS AND WEALTH TOGETHER.
NOW GO WE IN CONTENT TO LIBERTY, AND NOT TO BANISHMENT.

NOW, BROTHERS IN EXILE, ARE NOT THESE WOODS MORE FREE FROM PERIL THAN THE ENVIOUS COURT?
EVEN TILL I SHRINK WITH COLD, I SMILE AND SAY, "THIS IS NO FLATTERY: THESE ARE COUNSELLORS THAT FEELINGLY PERSUADE ME WHAT I AM."
SWEET ARE THE USES OF ADVERSITY: OUR LIFE FINDS TONGUES IN TREES, BOOKS IN THE RUNNING BROOKS, SERMONS IN STONES, AND GOOD IN EVERYTHING.

HAPPY IS YOUR GRACE, THAT CAN TRANSLATE THE STUBBORNNESS OF FORTUNE INTO SO SWEET A STYLE.
COME, SHALL WE GO AND KILL US VENISON?
AND YET IT IRKS ME, THE POOR DAPPLED FOOLS SHOULD IN THEIR OWN CONFINES HAVE THEIR HAUNCHES GORED.
INDEED, MY LORD, THE MELANCHOLY JAQUES GRIEVES AT THAT,
AND SWEARS YOU DO MORE USURP THAN DOTH YOUR BROTHER THAT HATH BANISHED YOU.

TODAY AMIENS AND MYSELF
DID STEAL BEHIND HIM
AS HE LAY UNDER AN OAK TO WHICH
A POOR SEQUESTERED STAG,
THAT FROM THE HUNTER'S
AIM HAD TAKEN A HURT...
DID COME TO LANGUISH.

BIG ROUND TEARS COURSED DOWN HIS INNOCENT NOSE...
AND THUS THE MELANCHOLY JAQUES STOOD AUGMENTING IT WITH TEARS.
DID HE NOT MORALIZE THIS SPECTACLE?
OH YES, INTO A THOUSAND SIMILES.

POOR DEER, THOU MAK'ST A TESTAMENT, GIVING THY SUM TO THAT WHICH HAD TOO MUCH.
ANON, A CARELESS HERD, FULL OF THE PASTURE, JUMPS ALONG BY HIM AND NEVER STAYS TO GREET HIM.
AY, SWEEP ON, YOU FAT AND GREASY CITIZENS!
WHEREFORE DO YOU LOOK UPON THAT POOR BANKRUPT THERE?

THUS MOST INVECTIVELY HE PIERCETH THROUGH THE BODY OF THE COUNTRY, CITY, COURT, YEA, AND OF THIS OUR LIFE...
SWEARING THAT WE ARE MERE USURPERS – TYRANTS – TO FRIGHT THE ANIMALS AND TO KILL THEM.
SHOW ME THE PLACE. I LOVE HIM IN THESE SULLEN FITS.

CAN IT BE POSSIBLE THAT NO MAN SAW THEM?
IT CANNOT BE!
SOME VILLAINS OF MY COURT ARE OF CONSENT IN THIS.
HER ATTENDANTS SAW HER ABED,
AND IN THE MORNING FOUND THE BED UNTREASURED OF THEIR MISTRESS.
MY LORD, THE CLOWN IS ALSO MISSING.

THE PRINCESS'S GENTLEWOMAN SECRETLY OVERHEARD...
YOUR DAUGHTER AND HER COUSIN MUCH COMMEND THE GRACES OF THE WRESTLER THAT DID LATELY FOIL THE SINEWY CHARLES.
SHE BELIEVES WHEREVER THEY ARE GONE THAT YOUTH IS SURELY IN THEIR COMPANY.
SEND TO HIS BROTHER.
I'LL MAKE HIM FIND HIM!

O MY GENTLE MASTER! WHAT MAKE YOU HERE?
YOUR PRAISE IS COME TOO SWIFTLY HOME BEFORE YOU.
YOUR VIRTUES ARE TRAITORS TO YOU.
O, WHAT A WORLD IS THIS!
WHY, WHAT'S THE MATTER?

YOUR BROTHER THIS NIGHT MEANS TO BURN THE LODGING –
AND YOU WITHIN IT.
I OVERHEARD HIM.
THIS HOUSE IS BUT A BUTCHERY.
DO NOT ENTER IT!
...
WHITHER WOULDST THOU HAVE ME GO?

WOULDST THOU HAVE ME BEG MY FOOD?
OR WITH A SWORD ENFORCE A THIEVISH LIVING ON THE COMMON ROAD?
I RATHER WILL SUBJECT ME TO THE MALICE OF A BLOODY BROTHER.
I HAVE FIVE HUNDRED CROWNS I SAVED UNDER YOUR FATHER.
ALL THIS I GIVE YOU.
LET ME BE YOUR SERVANT.
THOUGH I LOOK OLD, I'LL DO THE SERVICE OF A YOUNGER MAN.

O GOOD OLD MAN!
THOU ART NOT FOR THE FASHION OF THESE TIMES.
WE'LL GO ALONG TOGETHER –
AND ERE WE HAVE THY YOUTHFUL WAGES SPENT, WE'LL LIGHT UPON SOME SETTLED LOW CONTENT.
MASTER, I WILL FOLLOW THEE TO THE LAST GASP WITH TRUTH AND LOYALTY.
FORTUNE CANNOT RECOMPENSE ME BETTER...
THAN TO DIE WELL, AND NOT MY MASTER'S DEBTOR.

O JUPITER! HOW WEARY ARE MY SPIRITS!
I CARE NOT FOR MY SPIRITS IF MY LEGS WERE NOT WEARY.
I COULD FIND IT IN MY HEART TO DISGRACE MY MAN'S APPAREL AND CRY LIKE A WOMAN.
BUT I MUST COMFORT THE WEAKER VESSEL.
THEREFORE...

COURAGE, GOOD ALIENA!
I PRAY YOU, BEAR WITH ME. I CANNOT GO NO FURTHER.
I HAD RATHER BEAR WITH YOU THAN BEAR YOU.
WELL...
THIS IS THE FOREST OF AR-DEN.
AY, THE MORE FOOL I.
WHEN I WAS AT HOME, I WAS IN A BETTER PLACE.

LOOK YOU,
WHO COMES HERE?
O CORIN,
HOW I DO LOVE HER!
I PARTLY GUESS,
FOR I HAVE LOVED
ERE NOW.
NO, CORIN.
BEING OLD, THOU CANST
NOT GUESS.

HOW MANY ACTIONS MOST RIDICULOUS HAST THOU BEEN DRAWN TO BY THY FANTASY?
A THOUSAND THAT I HAVE FORGOTTEN.
IF THOU REMEMBER NOT THE SLIGHTEST FOLLY THAT EVER LOVE DID MAKE THEE RUN INTO...
THOU HAST NOT LOVED.
O PHOEBE!
PHOEBE! PHOEBE!
...
BAAAA

ALAS, POOR SHEPHERD!
SEARCHING OF THY WOUND, I HAVE FOUND MINE OWN.
AND I MINE.
I REMEMBER WHEN I WAS IN LOVE...
I BROKE MY SWORD UPON A STONE, AND BID HIM TAKE THAT FOR COMING A-NIGHT TO JANE SMILE!
WE THAT ARE TRUE LOVERS RUN INTO STRANGE CAPERS.
BUT AS ALL IS MORTAL, SO IS ALL LOVE FOLLY!

THOU SPEAK'ST WISER THAN THOU ART WARE OF.
NAY, I SHALL NEVER BE WARE OF MINE OWN WIT TILL I BREAK MY SHINS AGAINST IT.
GRAB!
I PRAY YOU, QUESTION YOND MAN, IF HE FOR GOLD WILL GIVE US ANY FOOD.
I FAINT ALMOST TO DEATH.

HOLLA, YOU CLOWN!
PEACE, FOOL, HE'S NOT THY KINSMAN.
SQUEEZE!
Ouch! Ouch!!
GOOD EVEN TO YOU, FRIEND.
AND TO YOU, GENTLE SIR, AND TO YOU ALL.

I PRITHEE, SHEPHERD, BRING US WHERE WE MAY REST OURSELVES AND FEED.
HERE'S A YOUNG MAID FAINTS FOR SUCCOUR.
FAIR SIR, I PITY HER, AND WISH MY FORTUNES WERE MORE ABLE TO RELIEVE HER.
BUT I AM SHEPHERD TO ANOTHER MAN, AND HIS FLOCKS ARE NOW ON SALE.

BY REASON OF HIS ABSENCE THERE IS NOTHING THAT YOU WILL FEED ON.
WHAT IS HE THAT SHALL BUY HIS FLOCK AND PASTURE?
THAT YOUNG SWAIN THAT YOU SAW HERE...
BUT LITTLE CARES FOR BUYING ANYTHING.
Sigh...
PHOEBE ...
Jump & Dash!!

I PRAY THEE, BUY THE COTTAGE, PASTURE AND THE FLOCK, AND PAY FOR IT OF US.
I LIKE THIS PLACE AND WILLINGLY COULD WASTE MY TIME IN IT.
GO WITH ME.
IF YOU LIKE THIS KIND OF LIFE,
I WILL BUY IT WITH YOUR GOLD RIGHT SUDDENLY.

♪ UNDER THE GREENWOOD TREE WHO LOVES TO LIE WITH ME...
AND TURN HIS MERRY NOTE UNTO THE SWEET BIRD'S THROAT...
♪ COME HITHER,
COME HITHER, COME HITHER!
HERE SHALL HE SEE NO ENEMY
BUT WINTER AND ROUGH WEATHER. ♪
MORE, I PRITHEE, MORE!
clap clap

IT WILL MAKE YOU MELANCHOLY, MONSIEUR JAQUES.
I CAN SUCK MELANCHOLY OUT OF A SONG, AS A WEASEL SUCKS EGGS.
MORE, MORE!
THE DUKE HATH BEEN ALL THIS DAY TO LOOK YOU.
AND I HAVE BEEN ALL THIS DAY TO AVOID HIM.
HE IS TOO DISPUTABLE FOR MY COMPANY.

I'LL GIVE YOU A VERSE THAT I MADE YESTERDAY IN DESPITE OF MY INVENTION.
IF IT DO COME TO PASS THAT ANY MAN TURN ASS, LEAVING HIS WEALTH AND EASE, A STUBBORN WILL TO PLEASE...
DUC-DA-ME,
...DUC-DA-ME,
DUC-DA-ME...?
HERE SHALL HE SEE GROSS FOOLS AS HE, AN IF HE WILL COME...

...TO MEEEEEEE
...
...
WHAT'S THAT "DUC-DA-ME"?
'TIS A GREEK INVOCATION TO CALL FOOLS INTO A CIRCLE.
I'LL GO SLEEP IF I CAN. IF I CANNOT, I'LL RAIL AGAINST ALL THE FIRST-BORN OF EGYPT.
AND I'LL GO SEEK THE DUKE.
HIS BANQUET IS PREPARED.

DEAR MASTER, I CAN GO NO FURTHER.
O, I DIE FOR FOOD!
WHY, ADAM! CHEER THYSELF A LITTLE.
COME, I WILL BEAR THEE TO SOME SHELTER.
THOU SHALT NOT DIE FOR LACK OF A DINNER...
IF THERE LIVE ANYTHING IN THIS DESERT.

WHY, HOW NOW, MONSIEUR!
WHAT A LIFE IS THIS,
THAT YOUR POOR FRIENDS MUST WOO YOUR COMPANY?
Boo!
Hee-Hee
WHAT, YOU LOOK MERRILY?

A FOOL!
?
I MET A FOOL IN THE FOREST WHO BASKED IN THE SUN...
"GOOD MORROW, FOOL," QUOTH I.
NO, SIR –
CALL ME NOT FOOL TILL HEAVEN HATH SENT ME FORTUNE.
HE DREW A DIAL FROM HIS POKE, AND, LOOKING ON IT WITH LACK-LUSTRE EYE...
SAYS VERY WISELY...
IT IS TEN O'CLOCK.

'TIS BUT AN HOUR AGO SINCE IT WAS NINE, AND AFTER ONE HOUR MORE 'TWILL BE ELEVEN.
弐
三
AND SO FROM HOUR TO HOUR WE RIPE AND RIPE...
AND THEN FROM HOUR TO HOUR WE ROT AND ROT...
四
五
六
AND THEREBY HANGS A TALE.

WHEN I DID HEAR THE MOTLEY FOOL SO DEEP-CONTEMPLATIVE...
I DID LAUGH AN HOUR BY HIS DIAL.
HAHAHAHAHA
O NOBLE FOOL!
A WORTHY FOOL!
MOTLEY'S THE ONLY WEAR.
WHAT FOOL IS THIS?
多谢

ONE THAT HATH BEEN A COURTIER...
AND IN HIS BRAIN HE HATH STRANGE PLACES CRAMMED WITH OBSERVATION, THE WHICH HE VENTS IN MANGLED FORMS.
O THAT I WERE A FOOL!
I AM AMBITIOUS FOR A MOTLEY COAT.
THOU SHALT HAVE ONE.

IT IS MY ONLY SUIT. I MUST HAVE LIBERTY AS LARGE AS THE WIND TO BLOW ON WHOM I PLEASE.
AND THEY THAT ARE MOST GALLED WITH MY FOLLY, THEY MOST MUST LAUGH.
GIVE ME LEAVE TO SPEAK MY MIND...
AND I WILL CLEANSE THE FOUL BODY OF THE INFECTED WORLD –
IF THEY WILL PATIENTLY RECEIVE MY MEDICINE.

FIE ON THEE!
I CAN TELL WHAT THOU WOULD DO.
WHAT WOULD I DO BUT GOOD?
MOST MISCHIEVOUS FOUL SIN IN CHIDING SIN!
FOR THOU THYSELF HAST BEEN A LIBERTINE AS SENSUAL AS THE BRUTISH STING ITSELF.
ALL THE SORES AND EVILS WOULDST THOU DISGORGE INTO THE GENERAL WORLD.

EVILS
SGORGE
AL WORLD.
WHAT WOMAN IN THE CITY DO I NAME THAT I SAY BEARS THE COST OF PRINCES ON UNWORTHY SHOULDERS?
WHO CAN SAY THAT I MEAN HER...
WHEN SUCH IS HER NEIGHBOUR?

OR WHAT IS HE
OF BASEST FUNCTION,
THINKING THAT
I MEAN HIM...
slap!
BUT THEREIN SUITS
HIS FOLLY TO THE METTLE
OF MY SPEECH?
HOW THEN?
WHAT THEN?
LET ME SEE
WHEREIN MY TONGUE
HATH WRONGED HIM.
RUSTLE
RUSTLE
BUT WHO
COMES HERE?

FORBEAR AND EAT NO MORE!
WHY, I HAVE ATE NONE YET.
ART THOU THUS BOLDENED BY DISTRESS? OR ELSE A RUDE DESPISER OF GOOD MANNERS?

THE THORNY POINT OF BARE DISTRESS HATH TAKEN FROM ME THE SHOW OF SMOOTH CIVILITY.
BUT FORBEAR, I SAY!
HE DIES THAT TOUCHES ANY OF THIS FRUIT.
WHAT WOULD YOU HAVE?
I ALMOST DIE FOR FOOD.

...
SIT DOWN AND FEED – AND WELCOME TO OUR TABLE.
SPEAK YOU SO GENTLY?
PARDON ME, I PRAY YOU.
I THOUGHT THAT ALL THINGS HAD BEEN SAVAGE HERE.
BUT WHATEVER YOU ARE, IF EVER YOU KNOW WHAT IT IS TO PITY AND BE PITIED...
I BLUSH, AND HIDE MY SWORD.

TRUE IS IT THAT WE HAVE SEEN BETTER DAYS.
THEREFORE SIT YOU DOWN AND TAKE WHAT HELP WE HAVE.
THERE IS AN OLD POOR MAN WHO AFTER ME HATH LIMPED IN PURE LOVE.
TILL HE BE FIRST SUFFICED, I WILL NOT TOUCH A BIT.
GO FIND HIM OUT...
AND WE WILL NOTHING WASTE TILL YOU RETURN.

THOU SEEST WE ARE NOT ALL ALONE UNHAPPY.
THIS UNIVERSAL THEATRE PRESENTS MORE WOEFUL PAGEANTS THAN THE SCENE WHEREIN WE PLAY IN.
ALL THE WORLD'S A STAGE, AND ALL THE MEN AND WOMEN MERELY PLAYERS.
THEY HAVE THEIR EXITS AND THEIR ENTRANCES, AND...

ONE MAN IN HIS TIME PLAYS MANY PARTS, HIS ACTS BEING SEVEN AGES.
AT FIRST THE INFANT, MEWLING AND PUKING IN THE NURSE'S ARMS.
THEN THE WHINING SCHOOL-BOY, CREEPING LIKE SNAIL UNWILLINGLY TO SCHOOL.

THEN THE LOVER,
SIGHING LIKE FURNACE,
WITH A WOEFUL BALLAD TO
HIS MISTRESS' EYEBROW.
THEN A SOLDIER,
SUDDEN AND QUICK IN QUARREL,
SEEKING THE BUBBLE REPUTATION
EVEN IN THE CANNON'S MOUTH.

AND THEN THE JUSTICE, IN FAIR ROUND BELLY, FULL OF WISE SAWS AND MODERN INSTANCES.
AND SO HE PLAYS HIS PART.
THE SIXTH AGE SHIFTS INTO THE LEAN AND SLIPPERED PANTALOON...
WITH SPECTACLES ON NOSE, HIS BIG MANLY VOICE TURNING AGAIN TOWARD CHILDISH TREBLE.

LAST SCENE OF ALL, THAT ENDS THIS HISTORY...
IS SECOND CHILDISHNESS AND MERE OBLIVION...
SANS TEETH, SANS EYES,
SANS TASTE,
SANS EVERYTHING.
SET DOWN YOUR VENERABLE BURDEN, AND LET HIM FEED.
I SCARCE CAN SPEAK TO THANK YOU...

BLOW, BLOW, THOU WINTER WIND, THOU ARE NOT SO UNKIND
AS MAN'S INGRATITUDE. HEY-HO, SING UNTO THE GREEN HOLLY...
IF YOU BE THE GOOD SIR ROWLAND'S SON – AS YOU HAVE WHISPERED YOU WERE – BE TRULY WELCOME HITHER.
I AM THE DUKE THAT LOVED YOUR FATHER.
GIVE ME YOUR HAND AND LET ME ALL YOUR FORTUNES UNDERSTAND.

NOT SEEN HIM SINCE?
SIR, THAT CANNOT BE.
LOOK TO IT! FIND OUT THY BROTHER WHERESOEVER HE IS.
BRING HIM, DEAD OR LIVING, WITHIN THIS TWELVEMONTH...
OR TURN THOU NO MORE IN OUR TERRITORY.

THY LANDS AND ALL THINGS DO WE SEIZE...
TILL THOU CANST QUIT THEE BY THY BROTHER'S MOUTH OF WHAT WE THINK AGAINST THEE.
O THAT YOUR HIGHNESS KNEW MY HEART IN THIS!
I NEVER LOVED MY BROTHER IN MY LIFE.
MORE VILLAIN THOU.
WELL, PUSH HIM OUT OF DOORS!
...!

O ROSALIND,
THESE TREES SHALL BE MY BOOKS...
AND IN THEIR BARKS MY THOUGHTS I'LL CHARACTER...
THAT EVERY EYE IN THIS FOREST SHALL SEE THY VIRTUE WITNESSED EVERYWHERE.
RUN, RUN, ORLANDO,
CARVE ON EVERY TREE THE FAIR, THE CHASTE AND UNEXPRESSIVE SHE!

HOW LIKE YOU THIS SHEPHERD'S LIFE, MASTER TOUCHSTONE?
TRULY, SHEPHERD, IT IS A VERY VILE LIFE.
HAST ANY PHILOSOPHY IN THEE, SHEPHERD?
NO MORE BUT THAT I KNOW THE PROPERTY OF RAIN IS TO WET, AND FIRE TO BURN, THAT GOOD PASTURE MAKES FAT SHEEP...
AND THAT A GREAT CAUSE OF THE NIGHT IS LACK OF THE SUN.
CLAP CLAP
SUCH A ONE IS A NATURAL PHILOSOPHER.

RUSTLE RUSTLE
HERE COMES YOUNG MASTER GANYMEDE, MY NEW MISTRESS'S BROTHER.
"FROM THE EAST TO WESTERN IND, NO JEWEL IS LIKE ROSALIND.
HER WORTH, BEING MOUNTED ON THE WIND...
THROUGH ALL THE WORLD BEARS ROSALIND..."

WOW!
THIS IS THE VERY FALSE GALLOP OF VERSES.
WHY DO YOU INFECT YOURSELF WITH THEM?
PEACE, YOU DULL FOOL! I FOUND THEM ON A TREE.
TRULY, THE TREE YIELDS BAD FRUIT.
HERE COMES MY SISTER READING. STAND ASIDE.

"NATURE PRESENTLY DISTILLED
HELEN'S CHEEK BUT NOT HER HEART,
CLEOPATRA'S MAJESTY,
ATALANTA'S BETTER PART,
SAD LUCRETIA'S MODESTY.
THUS ROSALIND OF MANY PARTS
BY HEAVENLY SYNOD WAS DEVISED..."
DIDST THOU HEAR
THESE VERSES?
grin♥
!

O, YES,
I HEARD THEM ALL,
AND MORE TOO.
TROW YOU WHO
HATH DONE THIS?
IS IT A MAN?
AND A CHAIN THAT
YOU ONCE WORE ABOUT
HIS NECK.
CHANGE YOU COLOUR?

...!
I PRITHEE NOW...
PULL!
WITH MOST PETITIONARY VEHEMENCE, TELL ME WHO IT IS.
O WONDERFUL, WONDERFUL, AND AGAIN WONDERFUL!
IT IS YOUNG ORLANDO, THAT TRIPPED UP THE WRESTLER'S HEELS AND YOUR HEART BOTH IN AN INSTANT.
ORLANDO?
ORLANDO.
Hee-hee

BUT DOTH HE KNOW
THAT I AM IN THIS FOREST
AND IN MAN'S APPAREL?
Go Away!
PUSH
PUSH
I FOUND HIM UNDER A TREE,
LIKE A DROPPED ACORN.
HE WAS FURNISHED
LIKE A HUNTER.
O, OMINOUS!
HE COMES TO KILL
MY HEART!
SOFT!
COMES HE
NOT HERE?

CHIT CHAT
CHIT CHAT
'TIS HE! SLINK BY AND NOTE HIM.
I THANK YOU FOR YOUR COMPANY BUT,
GOOD FAITH, I HAD AS LIEF BEEN MYSELF ALONE.
Twitch Twitch
AND SO HAD I,
BUT YET, FOR FASHION'S SAKE, I THANK YOU TOO FOR YOUR SOCIETY.

I PRAY YOU, MAR NO MORE TREES WITH WRITING LOVE-SONGS IN THEIR BARKS.
I PRAY YOU, MAR NO MORE OF MY VERSES WITH READING THEM ILL-FAVOUREDLY.
Sigh
ROSALIND IS YOUR LOVE'S NAME?
YES, JUST.

I DO NOT LIKE HER NAME.
THERE WAS NO THOUGHT OF PLEASING YOU WHEN SHE WAS CHRISTENED.
WHAT STATURE IS SHE OF?
JUST AS HIGH AS MY HEART.

YOU HAVE A NIMBLE WIT.
THE WORST FAULT YOU HAVE IS TO BE IN LOVE.
'TIS A FAULT I WILL NOT CHANGE FOR YOUR BEST VIRTUE.
I AM WEARY OF YOU.
SLAP!
I WAS SEEKING FOR A FOOL WHEN I FOUND YOU.
HE IS DROWNED IN THE BROOK. LOOK IN AND YOU SHALL SEE HIM.

THERE I SHALL SEE MINE OWN FIGURE.
WHICH I TAKE TO BE EITHER A FOOL OR A CIPHER.
...
...
I'LL TARRY NO LONGER WITH YOU.
FAREWELL, GOOD SIGNIOR LOVE.
I AM GLAD OF YOUR DEPARTURE.
ADIEU, GOOD MONSIEUR MELANCHOLY.

I PRAY YOU, WHAT IS'T O'CLOCK?
Sigh
THERE'S NO CLOCK IN THE FOREST.
THEN THERE IS NO TRUE LOVER IN THE FOREST –
ELSE SIGHING EVERY MINUTE AND GROANING EVERY HOUR WOULD DETECT THE LAZY FOOT OF TIME AS WELL AS A CLOCK.
AND WHY NOT "THE SWIFT FOOT OF TIME"?

WHERE DWELL YOU, PRETTY YOUTH?
WITH THIS SHEPHERDESS, MY SISTER, HERE IN THE SKIRTS OF THE FOREST.
ARE YOU NATIVE OF THIS PLACE?
YOUR ACCENT IS SOMETHING FINER THAN YOU COULD PURCHASE IN SO REMOVED A DWELLING.

THERE IS A MAN HAUNTS THE FOREST THAT ABUSES OUR YOUNG PLANTS...
WITH CARVING "ROSALIND" ON THEIR BARKS.
I SWEAR TO THEE, YOUTH, BY THE WHITE HAND OF ROSALIND...
I AM THAT UNFORTUNATE HE.
phew
BUT ARE YOU SO MUCH IN LOVE AS YOUR RHYMES SPEAK?
NEITHER RHYME NOR REASON CAN EXPRESS HOW MUCH.

LOVE IS...
MERELY A MADNESS AND DESERVES A WHIP AS MADMEN DO.
YET I PROFESS CURING IT BY COUNSEL.
I WOULD NOT BE CURED, YOUTH.
I WOULD CURE YOU...
IF YOU WOULD BUT CALL ME ROSALIND AND COME EVERY DAY TO WOO ME.

NOW, BY THE FAITH OF MY LOVE, I WILL.
GO WITH ME AND I'LL SHOW YOU.
AND YOU SHALL TELL ME WHERE IN THE FOREST YOU LIVE.
WITH ALL MY HEART, GOOD YOUTH.
NAY, YOU MUST CALL ME ROSALIND.

AUDREY, AM I THE MAN YET? DOTH MY SIMPLE FEATURE CONTENT YOU?
WHAT FEATURES?
I AM HERE WITH THEE AND THY GOATS...
AS THE POET OVID WAS AMONG THE GOTHS.
O KNOWLEDGE ILL-INHABITED, WORSE THAN JOVE IN A THATCHED HOUSE!

TRULY, I WOULD THE GODS HAD MADE THEE POETICAL.
I DO NOT KNOW WHAT "POETICAL" IS.
IS IT HONEST IN DEED AND WORD?
IS IT A TRUE THING?
TRUEST POETRY IS THE MOST FEIGNING — AS LOVERS DO FEIGN.

WOULD YOU NOT HAVE ME HONEST?
NO, TRULY, FOR HONESTY COUPLED TO BEAUTY IS HONEY TO SUGAR.
A MATERIAL FOOL!
WELL, I AM NOT FAIR,
AND THEREFORE I PRAY THE GODS MAKE ME HONEST.

BE IT AS IT MAY BE, I WILL MARRY THEE.
AND TO THAT END I HAVE BEEN WITH SIR OLIVER MARTEXT, THE VICAR OF THE NEXT VILLAGE...
Hi!
WHO HATH PROMISED TO MEET ME IN THIS PLACE AND TO COUPLE US.
I WOULD FAIN SEE THIS MEETING.
WELL, THE GODS GIVE US JOY!

HERE COMES SIR OLIVER.
WILL YOU DISPATCH US HERE UNDER THIS TREE?
OR SHALL WE GO WITH YOU TO YOUR CHAPEL?
IS THERE NONE HERE TO GIVE THE WOMAN?
TRULY SHE MUST BE GIVEN, OR THE MARRIAGE IS NOT LAWFUL.
PROCEED, I'LL GIVE HER.

GOOD MASTER WHAT-YE-CALL'T, HOW DO YOU, SIR?
WILL YOU BE MARRIED, MOTLEY?
AS THE OX HATH HIS BOW, SIR,
THE HORSE HIS CURB, AND THE FALCON HER BELLS...
SO MAN HATH HIS DESIRES.

AND WILL YOU BE MARRIED UNDER A BUSH LIKE A BEGGAR?
GET YOU TO CHURCH AND A GOOD PRIEST THAT CAN TELL YOU WHAT MARRIAGE IS.
I WERE BETTER TO BE MARRIED OF HIM, FOR HE IS NOT LIKE TO MARRY ME WELL...
?!
AND NOT BEING WELL MARRIED, IT WILL BE A GOOD EXCUSE FOR ME HEREAFTER TO LEAVE MY WIFE.

GO THOU WITH ME, AND LET ME COUNSEL THEE.
COME, SWEET AUDREY.
WE MUST BE MARRIED OR WE MUST LIVE IN BAWDRY.
FAREWELL, GOOD MASTER OLIVER...
WIND AWAY, BEGONE, I SAY...
I WILL NOT TO WEDDING WITH THEE.

WHY DID HE SWEAR HE WOULD COME THIS MORNING AND COMES NOT?
CERTAINLY, THERE IS NO TRUTH IN HIM.
DO YOU THINK SO? NOT TRUE IN LOVE?
YES — WHEN HE IS IN. BUT I THINK HE IS NOT IN.

YOU HAVE HEARD HIM SWEAR DOWNRIGHT HE WAS.
"WAS" IS NOT "IS". BESIDES, THE OATH OF A LOVER IS NO STRONGER THAN THE WORD OF A TAPSTER.
THEY ARE BOTH CONFIRMERS OF FALSE RECKONINGS.
HE ATTENDS HERE IN THE FOREST ON THE DUKE YOUR FATHER.

I MET THE DUKE YESTERDAY AND HAD MUCH QUESTION WITH HIM.
HE ASKED ME OF WHAT PARENTAGE I WAS.
MUNCH MUNCH
I TOLD HIM AS GOOD AS HE, SO HE LAUGHED AND LET ME GO.
BUT WHAT TALK WE OF FATHERS, WHEN THERE IS SUCH A MAN AS ORLANDO?
O, THAT'S A BRAVE MAN!
HE WRITES BRAVE VERSES, SPEAKS BRAVE WORDS, SWEARS BRAVE OATHS —
AND BREAKS THEM BRAVELY.
RUSTLE RUSTLE
WHO COMES HERE?

MISTRESS AND MASTER, YOU HAVE OFT ENQUIRED AFTER THE SHEPHERD THAT COMPLAINED OF LOVE,
PRAISING THE DISDAINFUL SHEPHERDESS THAT WAS HIS MISTRESS.
WELL, AND WHAT OF HIM?
IF YOU WILL SEE A PAGEANT TRULY PLAYED, I SHALL CONDUCT YOU.
...
THE SIGHT OF LOVERS FEEDETH THOSE IN LOVE.
BRING US TO THIS SIGHT.

SWEET PHOEBE, DO NOT SCORN ME.
SAY THAT YOU LOVE ME NOT, BUT SAY NOT SO IN BITTERNESS.
O FOR SHAME, TO SAY MINE EYES ARE MURDERERS!
SHOW THE WOUND MINE EYE HATH MADE IN THEE.
MINE EYES HURT THEE NOT, I AM SURE.
O DEAR PHOEBE,
YOU KNOW THE WOUNDS INVISIBLE THAT LOVE'S KEEN ARROWS MAKE.

YOU FOOLISH SHEPHERD, WHEREFORE DO YOU FOLLOW HER?
YOU ARE A THOUSAND TIMES A PROPERER MAN THAN SHE A WOMAN.
'TIS NOT HER GLASS BUT YOU THAT FLATTERS HER.
MISTRESS, DOWN ON YOUR KNEES!
AND THANK HEAVEN FOR A GOOD MAN'S LOVE.

FOR I MUST TELL YOU FRIENDLY IN YOUR EAR – SELL WHEN YOU CAN, YOU ARE NOT FOR ALL MARKETS.
CRY THE MAN MERCY, LOVE HIM, TAKE HIS OFFER!
SWEET YOUTH, I HAD RATHER HEAR YOU CHIDE THAN THIS MAN WOO.
WHY LOOK YOU SO UPON ME?

I PRAY YOU, DO NOT FALL IN LOVE WITH ME!
I AM FALSER THAN VOWS MADE IN WINE.
SHEPHERD, PLY HER HARD.
SHEPHERDESS, LOOK ON HIM BETTER, AND BE NOT PROUD.
NONE COULD BE SO ABUSED IN SIGHT AS HE.

KNOW'ST THOU THE YOUTH THAT SPOKE TO ME EREWHILE?
NOT VERY WELL, BUT HE HATH BOUGHT THE COTTAGE THAT OLD CORIN ONCE WAS MASTER OF.
THINK NOT I LOVE HIM THOUGH I ASK FOR HIM.
我的爱
I'LL WRITE TO HIM A VERY TAUNTING LETTER AND THOU SHALT BEAR IT.
WILT THOU, SILVIUS?
PHOEBE, WITH ALL MY HEART.

PRETTY YOUTH!
LET ME BE BETTER ACQUAINTED WITH THEE.
THEY SAY YOU ARE A MELANCHOLY FELLOW.
WHY, 'TIS GOOD TO BE SAD AND SAY NOTHING.
...
WHY THEN, 'TIS GOOD TO BE A POST.
HAHAHAHA

WHY, ORLANDO!
WHERE HAVE YOU BEEN
ALL THIS WHILE?
YOU A LOVER?
lover?
MY FAIR ROSALIND,
I COME WITHIN AN HOUR
OF MY PROMISE.
BREAK AN HOUR'S
PROMISE IN LOVE?
Whatever...
PARDON ME,
DEAR ROSALIND.
Bye!

...COME, WOO ME.
WHAT WOULD YOU SAY TO ME NOW,
IF I WERE YOUR VERY VERY ROSALIND?
I WOULD KISS BEFORE I SPOKE.
NAY, YOU WERE BETTER SPEAK FIRST.
WOW
WOW

HOW IF THE KISS BE DENIED?
AM NOT I YOUR ROSALIND?
I TAKE SOME JOY TO SAY YOU ARE,
BECAUSE I WOULD BE TALKING OF HER.
WELL, IN HER PERSON I SAY I WILL NOT HAVE YOU.

THEN
IN MINE OWN PERSON
I DIE.
THE POOR
WORLD IS...
ALMOST SIX
THOUSAND YEARS OLD.
IN ALL THIS TIME
MEN HAVE DIED AND WORMS
HAVE EATEN THEM,
BUT NOT FOR LOVE.
I WOULD NOT HAVE
MY RIGHT ROSALIND
OF THIS MIND,
FOR I PROTEST,
HER FROWN MIGHT
KILL ME.

OH...
I WILL BE YOUR ROSALIND IN A MORE COMING-ON DISPOSITION,
AND ASK ME WHAT YOU WILL, I WILL GRANT IT.
THEN LOVE ME, ROSALIND.
AND WILT THOU HAVE ME?
COME, SISTER, YOU SHALL BE THE PRIEST AND MARRY US.
PRAY THEE, MARRY US.
?

WILL YOU, ORLANDO...
HAVE TO WIFE THIS ROSALIND?
I WILL.
AY, BUT WHEN?
WHY NOW, AS FAST AS SHE CAN MARRY US.
THEN YOU MUST SAY, "I TAKE THEE, ROSALIND, FOR WIFE."

I TAKE THEE, ROSALIND,
FOR WIFE.
NOW TELL ME HOW LONG YOU WOULD HAVE HER AFTER YOU HAVE POSSESSED HER?
FOR EVER AND A DAY.
SAY "A DAY" WITHOUT THE "EVER".

!
NO, NO, ORLANDO, MEN ARE APRIL WHEN THEY WOO, DECEMBER WHEN THEY WED.
FOR THESE TWO HOURS, ROSALIND, I WILL LEAVE THEE.
I CANNOT LACK THEE TWO HOURS.
I MUST ATTEND THE DUKE AT DINNER. BY TWO O'CLOCK I WILL BE WITH THEE AGAIN.
IF YOU COME ONE MINUTE BEHIND YOUR HOUR...
I WILL THINK YOU MOST UNWORTHY OF HER YOU CALL ROSALIND.
BEWARE MY CENSURE AND KEEP YOUR PROMISE.
WITH NO LESS RELIGION THAN IF THOU WERT INDEED MY ROSALIND.

YOU HAVE MISUSED OUR SEX IN YOUR LOVE-PRATE!
O MY PRETTY LITTLE COZ...
THAT THOU DIDST KNOW HOW MANY FATHOM DEEP I AM IN LOVE!
SLAP!
OR RATHER BOTTOMLESS, THAT AS FAST AS YOU POUR AFFECTION IN, IT RUNS OUT.
I AM IN LOVE.
I'LL TELL THEE, ALIENA,
I CANNOT BE OUT OF THE SIGHT OF ORLANDO.
I'LL GO FIND A SHADOW AND SIGH TILL HE COME.

ZZZ...
!
MY GENTLE PHOEBE DID BID ME GIVE YOU THIS.
亲爱的
盖尼米得
WELL, SHEPHERD, WELL...
THIS IS A LETTER OF YOUR OWN DEVICE.
NO, I PROTEST, PHOEBE DID WRITE IT.
COME, COME, YOU ARE A FOOL.
I SAY SHE NEVER DID INVENT THIS LETTER.

TAP!
THIS IS A MAN'S INVENTION AND HIS HAND.
SURE, IT IS HERS.
WHY, 'TIS A BOISTEROUS AND A CRUEL STYLE.
WILL YOU HEAR THE LETTER?
SO PLEASE YOU, FOR I NEVER HEARD IT YET.
MARK HOW THE TYRANT WRITES...

"HE THAT BRINGS THESE LINES TO THEE LITTLE KNOWS THIS LOVE IN ME,
AND BY HIM SEAL UP THY MIND, WHETHER THAT THY YOUTH AND KIND...
WILL THE FAITHFUL OFFER TAKE OF ME AND ALL THAT I CAN MAKE, OR ELSE BY HIM MY LOVE DENY,
AND THEN I'LL STUDY HOW TO DIE."
ALAS, POOR SHEPHERD!

DO YOU PITY HIM?
NO, HE DESERVES NO PITY.
WILT THOU LOVE SUCH A WOMAN?
Nod Nod
WELL, GO YOUR WAY TO HER, AND SAY THIS TO HER.
IF SHE LOVE ME, I CHARGE HER TO LOVE THEE.
IF SHE WILL NOT, I WILL NEVER HAVE HER, UNLESS THOU ENTREAT FOR HER.
IF YOU BE A TRUE LOVER, HENCE, AND NOT A WORD.

PRAY YOU,
IF YOU KNOW...
WHERE IN
THIS FOREST STANDS
A SHEEPCOTE?
AT THIS HOUR
THE HOUSE DOTH
KEEP ITSELF.
THERE'S NONE
WITHIN.
ARE NOT YOU
THE OWNER OF
THE HOUSE I DID
ENQUIRE FOR?
IT IS NO BOAST
TO SAY WE ARE.

ORLANDO TO THAT YOUTH HE CALLS HIS ROSALIND...
SENDS THIS BLOODY NAPKIN.
ARE YOU HE?
I AM.
WHAT MUST WE UNDERSTAND BY THIS?
SOME OF MY SHAME...
IF YOU WILL KNOW OF ME WHAT MAN I AM,
AND HOW AND WHY AND WHERE THIS HANDKERCHIEF WAS STAINED.
I PRAY YOU, TELL IT.

WHEN LAST ORLANDO PARTED FROM YOU...
HE LEFT A PROMISE TO RETURN AGAIN WITHIN AN HOUR AND, PACING THROUGH THE FOREST,
LO, WHAT OBJECT DID PRESENT ITSELF!
UNDER AN OAK, A WRETCHED RAGGED MAN,
OVERGROWN WITH HAIR, LAY SLEEPING ON HIS BACK.

ABOUT HIS NECK
A SNAKE HAD
WREATHED ITSELF,
HER HEAD IN THREAT
APPROACHED THE OPENING
OF HIS MOUTH.
BUT SUDDENLY
SEEING ORLANDO,
...IT DID SLIP AWAY
INTO A BUSH.

UNDER WHICH BUSH
A LIONESS LAY COUCHING...
WITH CATLIKE WATCH,
WHEN THE SLEEPING MAN
SHOULD STIR.
THIS SEEN,
ORLANDO DID APPROACH
THE MAN...
AND FOUND IT WAS
HIS ELDER BROTHER.

I HAVE HEARD HIM SPEAK OF THAT SAME BROTHER,
AND HE DID RENDER HIM THE MOST UNNATURAL THAT LIVED AMONGST MEN.
AND WELL HE MIGHT SO DO...
FOR WELL I KNOW HE WAS UNNATURAL.
BUT TO ORLANDO - DID HE LEAVE HIM THERE, FOOD TO THE HUNGRY LIONESS?

TWICE DID HE TURN HIS BACK BUT KINDNESS,
NOBLER EVER THAN REVENGE...
MADE HIM GIVE BATTLE TO THE LIONESS...

IN WHICH HURTLING,
FROM MISERABLE SLUMBER I AWAKED.

ARE YOU HIS BROTHER?
WAS IT YOU HE RESCUED?
WAS IT YOU THAT DID SO OFT CONTRIVE TO KILL HIM?
'TWAS I, BUT 'TIS NOT I.
I DO NOT SHAME TO TELL YOU WHAT I WAS...
SINCE MY CONVERSION SO SWEETLY TASTES, BEING THE THING I AM.

HE LED ME TO THE GENTLE DUKE,
WHO GAVE ME FRESH ARRAY.
MY BROTHER LED ME TO HIS CAVE.
HERE, UPON HIS ARM, THE LIONESS HAD TORN SOME FLESH AWAY,
AND I BOUND UP HIS WOUND.

HE SENT ME HITHER, STRANGER AS I AM, TO TELL THIS STORY,
THAT YOU MIGHT EXCUSE HIS BROKEN PROMISE...
AND TO GIVE THIS NAPKIN, DYED IN HIS BLOOD, TO THE SHEPHERD YOUTH THAT HE IN SPORT DOTH CALL HIS ROSALIND.
WHY, HOW NOW, SWEET GANYMEDE!

BE OF GOOD CHEER, YOUTH.
YOU A MAN? YOU LACK A MAN'S HEART.
I DO SO, I CONFESS IT.
TELL YOUR BROTHER HOW WELL I COUNTERFEITED.
THIS WAS A PASSION OF EARNEST.
COUNTERFEIT, I ASSURE YOU.
WELL THEN, COUNTERFEIT TO BE A MAN.

SO I DO.
BUT IN FAITH, I SHOULD HAVE BEEN A WOMAN BY RIGHT.
YOU LOOK PALER AND PALER.
I MUST BEAR ANSWER BACK HOW YOU EXCUSE MY BROTHER... ROSALIND.
I SHALL DEVISE SOMETHING.
BUT, I PRAY YOU, COMMEND MY COUNTERFEITING TO HIM.

IS'T POSSIBLE THAT ON SO LITTLE ACQUAINTANCE YOU SHOULD LOVE HER?
AND LOVING, WOO? AND WOOING, SHE SHOULD GRANT?
I LOVE ALIENA.
CONSENT THAT WE MAY ENJOY EACH OTHER.
IT SHALL BE TO YOUR GOOD,
FOR MY FATHER'S HOUSE AND ALL THE REVENUE WILL I ESTATE UPON YOU...
AND HERE LIVE AND DIE A SHEPHERD.
YOU HAVE MY CONSENT.

GO AND PREPARE ALIENA,
FOR HERE COMES MY ROSALIND.
Hi
O MY DEAR ORLANDO, HOW IT GRIEVES ME TO SEE THEE WEAR THY HEART IN A SCARF.
IT IS MY ARM.
I THOUGHT THY HEART HAD BEEN WOUNDED WITH THE CLAWS OF A LION.
WOUNDED IT IS, BUT WITH THE EYES OF A LADY.

DID YOUR BROTHER TELL YOU HOW I COUNTERFEITED TO SWOON
WHEN HE SHOWED ME YOUR HANDKERCHIEF?
AHHHH
AY, AND GREATER WONDERS THAN THAT.
O, I KNOW.
FOR YOUR BROTHER AND MY SISTER NO SOONER MET
BUT THEY LOVED, AND MADE A PAIR OF STAIRS TO MARRIAGE.

THEY SHALL BE MARRIED TOMORROW.
BUT O, HOW BITTER A THING IT IS TO LOOK INTO HAPPINESS THROUGH ANOTHER MAN'S EYES!
I SHALL THINK MY BROTHER HAPPY IN HAVING WHAT HE WISHES FOR.
BELIEVE THEN THAT I CAN DO STRANGE THINGS.
I HAVE, SINCE I WAS THREE YEARS OLD, CONVERSED WITH A MAGICIAN.
IF YOU DO LOVE ROSALIND, SHALL YOU MARRY HER.

IT IS NOT IMPOSSIBLE TO ME TO SET HER BEFORE YOUR EYES TOMORROW,
HUMAN AS SHE IS, AND WITHOUT ANY DANGER.
SPEAK'ST THOU IN SOBER MEANINGS?
I AM A MAGICIAN.
IF YOU WILL BE MARRIED TOMORROW, YOU SHALL,
AND TO ROSALIND, IF YOU WILL.
LOOK, HERE COMES A LOVER OF MINE, AND A LOVER OF HERS.

YOUTH, YOU HAVE DONE ME MUCH UNGENTLENESS TO SHOW THE LETTER THAT I WRIT TO YOU.
I CARE NOT IF I HAVE.
YOU ARE THERE FOLLOWED BY A FAITHFUL SHEPHERD.
LOOK UPON HIM, LOVE HIM; HE WORSHIPS YOU.
GOOD SHEPHERD, TELL THIS YOUTH WHAT 'TIS TO LOVE.

IT IS TO BE ALL MADE OF SIGHS AND TEARS...
AND SO AM I FOR PHOEBE.
AND I FOR GANYMEDE.
AND I FOR ROSALIND.
AND I FOR NO WOMAN.
PRAY YOU, NO MORE OF THIS.

TOMORROW MEET ME ALL TOGETHER.
I WILL MARRY YOU, IF EVER I MARRY WOMAN,
AND I'LL BE MARRIED TOMORROW.
I WILL SATISFY YOU, IF EVER I SATISFIED MAN,
AND YOU SHALL BE MARRIED TOMORROW.
I WILL CONTENT YOU, IF WHAT PLEASES YOU CONTENTS YOU,
AND YOU SHALL BE MARRIED TOMORROW.

AS YOU LOVE ROSALIND, MEET.
AS YOU LOVE PHOEBE, MEET.
AND AS I LOVE NO WOMAN, I'LL MEET.
SO, FARE YOU WELL. I HAVE LEFT YOU COMMANDS.
I'LL NOT FAIL, IF I LIVE.
NOR I.
NOR I.

TOMORROW IS THE JOYFUL DAY, AUDREY.
TOMORROW WILL WE BE MARRIED.
I DO DESIRE IT WITH ALL MY HEART...
AND I HOPE IT IS NO DISHONEST DESIRE...
TO DESIRE TO BE A WOMAN OF THE WORLD?

DOST THOU BELIEVE, ORLANDO,
THE BOY CAN DO ALL THAT HE PROMISED?
I SOMETIMES DO BELIEVE...
AND SOMETIMES DO NOT.
YOU SAY, IF I BRING IN YOUR ROSALIND,
YOU WILL BESTOW HER ON ORLANDO HERE?
THAT WOULD I, HAD I KINGDOMS TO GIVE WITH HER.

KEEP YOU YOUR WORD, O DUKE,
TO GIVE YOUR DAUGHTER.
YOU YOURS, ORLANDO,
TO RECEIVE HIS DAUGHTER.
KEEP YOUR WORD, PHOEBE,
THAT YOU'LL MARRY ME, OR ELSE, REFUSING ME, TO WED THIS SHEPHERD.
KEEP YOUR WORD, SILVIUS,
THAT YOU'LL MARRY HER, IF SHE REFUSE ME.
AND FROM HENCE I GO...
TO MAKE THESE DOUBTS ALL EVEN.

I DO REMEMBER IN THIS SHEPHERD BOY
SOME LIVELY TOUCHES OF MY DAUGHTER'S FAVOUR.
MY LORD, THE FIRST TIME THAT I EVER SAW HIM,
METHOUGHT HE WAS A BROTHER TO YOUR DAUGHTER.
BUT THIS BOY IS FOREST-BORN, AND HATH BEEN TUTORED BY HIS UNCLE,
WHOM HE REPORTS TO BE A GREAT MAGICIAN, OBSCURED IN THE CIRCLE OF THIS FOREST.

HERE COMES A PAIR OF VERY STRANGE BEASTS...
WHICH IN ALL TONGUES ARE CALLED FOOLS.
SALUTATION AND GREETING TO YOU ALL!
THIS IS THE MOTLEY-MINDED GENTLEMAN
THAT I HAVE SO OFTEN MET IN THE FOREST.
I LIKE HIM VERY WELL.

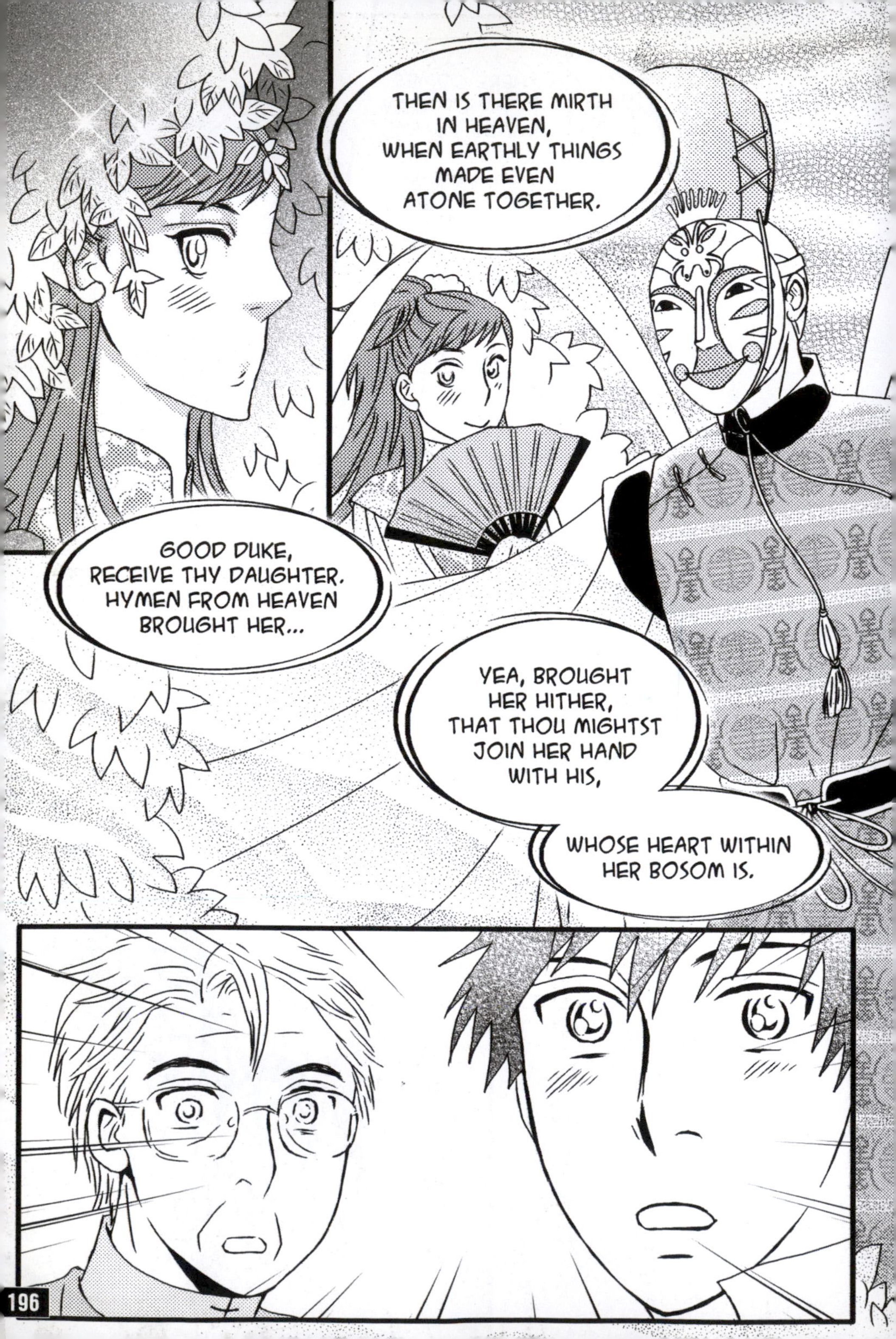
THEN IS THERE MIRTH IN HEAVEN, WHEN EARTHLY THINGS MADE EVEN ATONE TOGETHER.
GOOD DUKE, RECEIVE THY DAUGHTER. HYMEN FROM HEAVEN BROUGHT HER...
YEA, BROUGHT HER HITHER, THAT THOU MIGHTST JOIN HER HAND WITH HIS,
WHOSE HEART WITHIN HER BOSOM IS.

TO YOU
I GIVE MYSELF,
FOR I AM YOURS.
TO YOU
I GIVE MYSELF,
FOR I AM YOURS.
IF THERE BE
TRUTH IN SIGHT,
YOU ARE
MY DAUGHTER.
IF THERE BE
TRUTH IN SIGHT,
YOU ARE
MY ROSALIND.
IF SIGHT
AND SHAPE
BE TRUE,
WHY THEN,
MY LOVE
ADIEU!

PEACE, HO!
I BAR CONFUSION.
'TIS I MUST MAKE CONCLUSION
OF THESE MOST STRANGE EVENTS.
HERE'S EIGHT
THAT MUST TAKE HANDS...
TO JOIN IN
HYMEN'S BANDS,
IF TRUTH HOLDS
TRUE CONTENTS.

YOU AND YOU
NO CROSS
SHALL PART.
YOU AND YOU
ARE HEART IN HEART.
YOU TO HIS LOVE
MUST ACCORD,
OR HAVE
A WOMAN TO
YOUR LORD.
YOU AND YOU
ARE SURE TOGETHER
AS THE WINTER TO
FOUL WEATHER.

I AM THE SECOND SON OF OLD SIR ROWLAND THAT BRING THESE TIDINGS TO THIS FAIR ASSEMBLY.
DUKE FREDERICK, HEARING HOW THAT EVERY DAY MEN OF GREAT WORTH RESORTED TO THIS FOREST...
ADDRESSED A MIGHTY POWER IN HIS OWN CONDUCT,
PURPOSELY TO TAKE HIS BROTHER HERE AND PUT HIM TO THE SWORD.

TO THIS WILD WOOD HE CAME, WHERE, MEETING WITH AN OLD RELIGIOUS MAN,
WAS CONVERTED BOTH FROM HIS ENTERPRISE AND FROM THE WORLD...
HIS CROWN BEQUEATHING TO HIS BANISHED BROTHER,
AND ALL THEIR LANDS RESTORED TO THEM THAT WERE WITH HIM EXILED.
WELCOME, YOUNG MAN.

THOU OFFER'ST FAIRLY TO THY BROTHERS' WEDDING.
EVERY OF THIS HAPPY NUMBER SHALL SHARE THE GOOD OF OUR RETURNED FORTUNE,
ACCORDING TO THE MEASURE OF THEIR STATES...
MEANTIME, FORGET THIS NEW-FALLEN DIGNITY AND FALL INTO OUR RUSTIC REVELRY.

IF I HEARD YOU RIGHTLY, THE DUKE HATH PUT ON A RELIGIOUS LIFE...
AND THROWN INTO NEGLECT THE POMPOUS COURT?
HE HATH.
TO HIM WILL I.
OUT OF THESE CONVERTITES THERE IS MUCH MATTER TO BE HEARD AND LEARNED.

STAY, JAQUES, STAY.
TO SEE NO PASTIME, I.
I'LL STAY AT YOUR ABANDONED CAVE.
PROCEED, PROCEED!
WE WILL BEGIN THESE RITES, AS WE DO TRUST THEY'LL END, IN TRUE DELIGHTS.

I CHARGE YOU, O WOMEN,
FOR THE LOVE YOU BEAR TO MEN, TO LIKE AS MUCH OF THIS PLAY AS PLEASE YOU.
AND I CHARGE YOU, O MEN,
FOR THE LOVE YOU BEAR TO WOMEN, THAT THE PLAY MAY PLEASE.
WHEN I MAKE CURTSY...
BID ME FAREWELL.
終劇

PLOT SUMMARY OF AS YOU LIKE IT

There has been a palace coup: Duke Frederick has banished his brother, Duke Senior, and now rules in his place, while Senior and his followers establish a "court-in-exile" in the Forest of Ar-Den. Meanwhile Orlando has been dispossessed of his inheritance by his bullying brother Oliver. When Orlando takes part in a wrestling match at court, Oliver persuades the champion to break his neck. Against the odds, Orlando wins – and sets the rest of the story in train.

Among the spectators are Duke Senior's daughter Rosalind and her best friend (and Duke Frederick's daughter) Celia. Rosalind and Orlando fall head over heels in love. Then disaster strikes: Duke Frederick banishes Rosalind, and Orlando is warned to flee the court as well.

Accompanied by his father's servant Adam, who informs him of Oliver's murderous intentions, Orlando sets off into the forest. Celia has meanwhile volunteered to share her cousin's exile, and suggests they should join Duke Senior, travelling incognito to avoid detection. Attended by Touchstone, their faithful Fool, Rosalind disguises herself as "Ganymede", a young man, with Celia posing as "his" sister. Both sets of travellers find hospitality in Ar-Den: Orlando and Adam are welcomed to Senior's table, while Rosalind, Celia, and Touchstone meet the honest shepherd Corin – and learn of young Silvius's unrequited love for Phoebe.

But Orlando is pining for his lost love, posting poetic celebrations of her on the forest trees – some of which are found by Rosalind herself, who, in her male disguise, approaches Orlando, offering to ease his heart by "impersonating" Rosalind. Love is elsewhere in the air: Touchstone has fallen for goat-herd Audrey; and when "Ganymede" (alias Rosalind) chides Phoebe for her rejection of Silvius, Phoebe promptly falls in love with "him".

The mood darkens when Oliver arrives with a bloody cloth: Orlando has been wounded saving Oliver from a lion, and is late for an appointment with "Ganymede". Oliver, shamed by Orlando's actions, is now a reformed character and duly falls in love with Celia.

Orlando arrives but can no longer continue the charade: Ganymede's impersonation of Rosalind is making him miss her all the more. "Ganymede" replies that Orlando and Rosalind will join Oliver and Celia at the altar. When Silvius and Phoebe arrive, "Ganymede" promises Phoebe that if "he" marries any woman, it will be her – but if "he" marries no woman, Phoebe must marry Silvius. Phoebe agrees.

And so the stage is set for four weddings – and an abstention. For while Audrey and Touchstone, Phoebe and Silvius, Celia and Oliver, and Rosalind and Orlando all tie the knot, the melancholy Jaques joins the now-penitent Duke Frederick in monastic contemplation.

A BRIEF LIFE OF WILLIAM SHAKESPEARE

Shakespeare's birthday is traditionally said to be the 23rd of April – St George's Day, patron saint of England. A good start for England's greatest writer. But that date and even his name are uncertain. He signed his own name in different ways. "Shakespeare" is now the accepted one out of dozens of different versions.

He was born at Stratford-upon-Avon in 1564, and baptized on 26th April. His mother, Mary Arden, was the daughter of a prosperous farmer. His father, John Shakespeare, a glove-maker, was a respected civic figure – and probably also a Catholic. In 1570, just as Will began school, his father was accused of illegal dealings. The family fell into debt and disrepute.

Will attended a local school for eight years. He did not go to university. The next ten years are a blank filled by suppositions. Was he briefly a Latin teacher, a soldier, a sea-faring explorer? Was he prosecuted and whipped for poaching deer?

We do know that in 1582 he married Anne Hathaway, eight years his senior, and three months pregnant. Two more children – twins – were born three years later but, by around 1590, Will had left Stratford to pursue a theatre career in London. Shakespeare's apprenticeship began as an actor and "pen for hire".

He learned his craft the hard way. He soon won fame as a playwright with often-staged popular hits.

He and his colleagues formed a stage company, the Lord Chamberlain's Men, which built the famous Globe Theatre. It opened in 1599 but was destroyed by fire in 1613 during a performance of *Henry VIII* which used gunpowder special effects. It was rebuilt in brick the following year.

Shakespeare was a financially successful writer who invested his money wisely in property. In 1597, he bought an enormous house in Stratford, and in 1608 became a shareholder in London's Blackfriars Theatre. He also redeemed the family's honour by acquiring a personal coat of arms.

Shakespeare wrote over 40 works, including poems, "lost" plays and collaborations, in a career spanning nearly 25 years. He retired to Stratford in 1613, where he died on 23rd April 1616, aged 52, apparently of a fever after a "merry meeting" of drinks with friends. Shakespeare did in fact die on St George's Day! He was buried "full 17 foot deep" in Holy Trinity Church, Stratford, and left an epitaph cursing anyone who dared disturb his bones.

There have been preposterous theories disputing Shakespeare's authorship. Some claim that Sir Francis Bacon (1561–1626), philosopher and Lord Chancellor, was the real author of Shakespeare's plays. Others propose Edward de Vere, Earl of Oxford (1550–1604), or, even more weirdly, Queen Elizabeth I. The implication is that the "real" Shakespeare had to be a university graduate or an aristocrat. Nothing less would do for the world's greatest writer.

Shakespeare is mysteriously hidden behind his work. His life will not tell us what inspired his genius.

MANGA SHAKESPEARE®

EDITORIAL

Richard Appignanesi: Text Adaptor

Richard Appignanesi was a founder and co-director of the Writers & Readers Publishing Cooperative and Icon Books where he originated the internationally acclaimed *Introducing* series. His own best-selling titles in the series include *Freud*, *Postmodernism* and *Existentialism*. He is also the author of the fiction trilogy *Italia Perversa* and the novel *Yukio Mishima's Report to the Emperor*. Currently associate editor of the journal *Third Text* and reviews editor of the journal *Futures*, his latest book *What do Existentialists Believe?* was released in 2006.

Nick de Somogyi: Textual Consultant

Nick de Somogyi works as a freelance writer and researcher, as a genealogist at the College of Arms, and as a contributing editor to *New Theatre Quarterly*. He is the founding editor of the *Globe Quartos* series, and was the visiting curator at Shakespeare's Globe, 2003–6. His publications include *Shakespeare's Theatre of War* (1998), *Jokermen and Thieves: Bob Dylan and the Ballad Tradition* (1986), and (from 2001) the *Shakespeare Folios* series for Nick Hern Books. He has also contributed to the Open University (1995), Carlton Television (2000), and BBC Radio 3 and Radio 4.

ARTIST

Chie Kutsuwada

Chie Kutsuwada is a member of UMISEN-YAMASEN, a group of young Japanese Manga artists based in London. Chie's work is often cute, cool, funny and always unique and original. She has contributed to many exhibitions in London and her first solo exhibition was in 2003 at London's Window Gallery. In 2005 Chie won The Royal College of Art Society and Thames & Hudson Art Book Prize and the Printmakers Council Award. In 2007 she was a finalist in The Embassy of Japan's national Manga Jiman competition. Chie draws digitally using a graphics tablet and had an extended piece of manga published in *The Mammoth Book of Best New Manga 2* (2007).

PUBLISHER

SelfMadeHero is a UK-based manga and graphic novel imprint, reinventing some of the most important works of European and world literature. In 2008 SelfMadeHero was named **UK Young Publisher of the Year** at the prestigious British Book Industry Awards.

OTHER TITLES IN THIS SERIES INCLUDE

Much Ado About Nothing, *King Lear*, *Henry VIII*, *Twelfth Night*, *The Merchant of Venice* and *The Taming of the Shrew*.

www.selfmadehero.com